Leader's Guide for group study

Be Joyful

Warren W. Wiersbe

Leader's Guide prepared by
DAVID R. DOUGLASS

Twelfth printing, 1989

VICTOR BOOKS
A DIVISION OF SCRIPTURE PRESS PUBLICATIONS INC.
USA CANADA ENGLAND

ISBN: 0-88207-918-2
© 1974 by SP Publications, Inc. All rights reserved
Printed in the United States of America

General Preparation

Survey the entire *Text* and this *Leader's Guide*. *This is basic.* Underline important passages in the text and make notes as ideas come to you, before you forget them. Become familiar with the entire course, including all units in the *Guide* that you will be using in your study. A general knowledge of what is coming up later will enable you to conduct each session more effectively and to keep discussion relevant to the subject at hand. If questions are asked that will be considered later in the course, postpone discussion until that time.

Add to your teaching notes any material and ideas you think important or of special help to your class. As teacher, your enthusiasm for the subject and your personal interest in those you teach, will in large measure determine the interest and response of your class.

We recommend strongly that you plan to use teaching aids, even if you merely jot down a word or two on a chalkboard from time to time to impress a point on the class. When you ask for a number of answers to a question, as in brainstorming, always jot down each answer in capsule form, to keep all ideas before the group. If no chalkboard is available, use a magic marker on large sheets of newsprint over a suitable easel. A printer can supply such paper for you at modest cost.

Once you have decided what visual or audio aids you will use, make sure *all* the necessary equipment is on hand *before* classtime. If you use electrical equipment such as a projector or recorder, make sure you have an extension cord available if needed. For chalkboards, have chalk and eraser. That's obvious, of course, but small details are easily forgotten.

Encourage class members to bring Bibles or New Testaments to class and use them. It is good to have several modern-speech translations on hand for purposes of comparison.

Getting Started Right

Start on time. This is especially important for the first session for two reasons. First, it will set the pattern for the rest of the course. If you begin the first lesson late, members will have less reason for being on time at the others. Those who are punctual will be robbed of time, and those who are habitually late will come still later next time. Second, the first session should begin promptly because getting acquainted, explaining the procedure, and introducing the textbook will shorten your study time as it is.

Begin with prayer, asking the Holy Spirit to open hearts and minds, to give understanding, and to apply the truths that are studied. The Holy Spirit is the great Teacher. No teaching, however orthodox and carefully presented, can be truly Christian or spiritual without His control.

Involve everyone. The suggested plans for each session provide a maximum of participation for members of your class. This is important because—
1. People are usually more interested if they take part.
2. People remember more of what they discuss together than they do of what they are told by a lecturer.
3. People like to help arrive at conclusions and applications. They are more likely to act on truth if they apply it to themselves than if it is applied to them by someone else.

To promote relaxed involvement, you may find it wise to—
1. Have the class sit in a circle or semicircle. Some who are not used to this idea may feel uncomfortable at first, but the arrangement makes class members feel more at home. It will also make discussion easier and more relaxed.
2. Remain seated while you teach (unless the class numbers over 25).
3. Be relaxed in your own attitude and manner. Remember that the class is not "yours," but the Lord's, so don't get tense!
4. Use some means to get the class better acquainted, unless all are well known to each other. At the first meeting or two each member could wear a large-lettered name tag. Each one might also briefly tell something about himself, and perhaps tell what, specifically, he expects to get from this study.

Adapting the Course

This material is designed for quarterly use on a weekly basis, but it may be readily adapted to different uses. Those who wish to teach the course over a 12 or 13 week period may simply follow the lesson arrangement as it is given in this *Guide,* using or excluding review/examination sessions as desired.

For 10 sessions, the class may combine four of the shorter lessons into two. The same procedure should be followed for five sessions. However, if the material is to be covered in five sessions, each one should be two hours long with a 10-minute break near the middle. Divide the text chapters among the sessions as needed.

An Alternate Approach

The lesson plans outlined for each session in this *Guide* assume that class members are reading their texts before each class meets. The teacher should make every effort to spark interest in the text by giving members provocative assignments (as suggested under each session) and by such methods as reading aloud an especially fascinating passage (very brief) from the next week's text.

When for any reason, most of the class members will *not* have read the text in advance, (as when the class meets each evening in Vacation Bible School and members work during the day, or as in the first session, when texts may not have been available previously), a slightly different procedure must be followed.

At the beginning of the period, divide the class into small study groups of from four to six persons. Don't separate couples. It is not necessary for the same individuals to be grouped together each time the class meets—though if members prefer this, by all means allow them to meet together regularly.

As teacher of the class, lead one of the study groups yourself. Appoint a leader for each of the other groups. If people are reluctant to be leaders, explain that they need not teach and that they need no advance knowledge of the subject.

Allow the groups and their leaders as much as half an hour to study the textbook together. Then reassemble the class. Ask leaders to report findings or questions of unusual interest or that provoked disagreement. Ask the class the questions you want discussed, and allow questions from your students. Be sure to summarize, in closing, what has been studied. Finally, urge each member of the class to make some specific application of the lesson to his life. Use any of the material in this *Guide* that is appropriate and for which you have time.

SESSION 1

The Joy Stealers / Text, Chapter 1

Session Goals
1. To help members of the class become better acquainted with one another and with you as their teacher. A group learns better and functions more effectively when those belonging to it know and understand each other.
2. To familiarize class members with the text, *Be Joyful,* and with the procedure you intend to follow during this course.
3. To motivate your class members to study outside of class (this is, of course, restricted when sessions are held on consecutive days) and to participate in class. People learn better when they *want to,* and especially when they participate in the process.
4. To increase and deepen knowledge of God's Word through careful and concerned study of Philippians. To learn from this study more of what genuine Christian joy is all about.

Preparation
Read through (or at least carefully scan) the entire text to get an overview and "feel" of the book. Study chapter 1 carefully, making notes as you read.

If you have not already done so, study pages 2-4 of this study guide carefully. Also familiarize yourself with the teaching methods described on the inside front and back covers.

You will discover that the first chapter of the text is an introduction to the whole book. It focuses on three central aspects of Christian joy: hindrances, aids, and practice.

Presentation
The first class session tends to set the mood for the whole study. You will, therefore, want to take special care that this session is carefully prepared and that your attitude, as well as methods, will reflect the kind of joy that is the theme of the course.

After prayer and any introductory remarks you may want to make, ask, *Just what is Christian joy, and how does it differ from ordinary happiness?* (Answers will vary, of course, but hopefully they will include the idea that Christian joy is God-given, it is only available to believers, it is influenced but not controlled by what happens to us, it is on a deeper and more constant level than ordinary happiness.)

Next you may want to compare briefly the lives and circumstances of Mark Twain and the Apostle Paul. Make up your own questions that will encourage discussion of these two very different individuals, bringing out how Twain, though highly popular and successful as a humorist was actually extremely unhappy, while Paul, though constantly criticized and persecuted, was also constantly joyful.

Ask, *How* (see *Text,* p. 18) *does "outlook determine outcome"?* (Dr. Wiersbe is not advocating a superficial power-of-positive-thinking philosophy; but he is speaking about inner rather than outer conditions. If our spiritual attitude is centered on Christ's principles, power, and promises, our spiritual condition will always be healthy and joyful.)

The first major section of the chapter deals with what the author calls "thieves of joy." Divide your class into four groups (or, if the class is large, into four sets of groups). Have each group discuss briefly one of the four "thieves," adding ideas and insights (including personal experiences) to what the text offers. After several minutes, have a representative from each group report its ideas to the class.

The next section of the chapter focuses on the four attitudes mentioned in Philippians that promote Christian joy. This is the heart of the chapter and, in many ways, lays the foundation for the rest of the study.

Have the class turn to Philippians 1. Ask someone to read verse 21; then have someone read James 1:8. *How does Paul describe the single-mindedness that James mentions?* (It is having all of one's life centered on Jesus Christ. Everything we think, plan, do, hope for takes its meaning and purpose from our Lord.)

Does a single-minded person simply ignore the circumstances in which he finds himself, acting as if they didn't exist? (No, single-mindedness isn't dishonest or unreal. But it looks at and interprets all circumstances in light of Christ—rather than the other way around, as we are often tempted to do; see *Text,* p. 19).

If time permits, you may want to use chalkboard 1 as you expand on the nature of spiritual single-mindedness.

The emphasis of Philippians 2 is on others, primarily other Christians, and the main attitude discussed is submissiveness. *Why is the submissive Christian not frustrated and aggravated easily?* (Because his main concern is not to serve or please himself but to please Christ and to serve others in His name. The problems that frustrate us the most are those

CHARACTERISTICS OF THE SINGLE MIND		
1:1-11	1:12-26	1:27-30

Chalkboard 1
Ask class members to look for specific characteristics of the single mind that are mentioned in the passages indicated. Write answers on board as they are given.

which interfere with our selfish interests. See *Text,* pp. 19-20.)

As a special feature this session, you may want to ask four members of the class to prepare *brief* reports on the four men suggested as outstanding examples of the submissive mind (*Text,* p. 20). A Bible dictionary would be a good resource for the reporters to use. They should concentrate on incidents or attitudes that especially reflect submissiveness.

Philippians 3 focuses on what Dr. Wiersbe calls the spiritual mind. *What kind of "things"* (3:19) *are unbelievers and unspiritual Christians most concerned about?* (Earthly things—which includes some necessary but secondary things such as food, clothing, shelter. But from the first part of verse 19, Paul obviously has in mind things which are specifically and always sinful, though he doesn't list them by name.)

Why can things, even potentially good things, never bring satisfaction and joy? (Because, since he is made in God's image and for God's purposes, man simply is not "programmed" to be satisfied with anything less than God—no matter how much Satan leads him to think otherwise. If someone else does not do so, you may want to mention Augustine's famous saying, "Thou hast made us for Thyself, and our souls are restless till they find their rest in Thee.") Ask the class to suggest ways, in addition to those given in the text, that the words *count* (3:7, 8, 13), *press* (3:14), and *look* (3:20) express the healthy, active spiritual mind.

Philippians 4 stresses the secure mind. *Why is worry* (see the "thieves" of joy studied earlier) *the great enemy of the secure mind?* (Worry is a type of fear, which by definition involves danger or insecurity or at least the feelings of danger or insecurity. Peace of mind—the basic characteristic of mental security—cannot coexist with worry.)

How you handle the last section of chapter 1 ("What Should We Do?") will depend on the particular needs of your class. If you have reason to believe any are not Christians, concentrate on part 1, "Be sure you are a Christian" (p. 22). In the time available, make the Gospel as clear as possible and give opportunity for receiving Christ as Saviour.

Assignment
Read chapter 2 of the text.

SESSION 2

How to Get Along with Christians / Text, Chapter 2

Session Goals
1. To discover the deeper, spiritual levels of Christian fellowship.
2. To grow personally in our own relations with fellow believers.

Preparation
Study and make notes on chapter 2 of the text, noting especially the different meanings, characteristics, and levels of fellowship. The focus of this session, as the title implies, is the relationship of Christians to each other. If believers cannot get along with one another, they cannot possibly have an effective witness to the world. If unbelievers cannot see how the Gospel makes Christians better, they will see little reason for accepting it for themselves.

If you know of particular problems between any of your class members, you may want to emphasize—without putting anyone on the spot—the parts of chapter 2 that apply most directly to this problem area.

Presentation
Before class begins, write on the board, *Fellowship is* . . . . After prayer and introduction of any new members that may be present, ask for definitions of fellowship with which to finish the statement on the board (see chalkboard 2). Mention that this question has to do with fellowship in general. After these suggestions are given, write on the board, *Christian fellowship is* . . . , and ask for ways that Christian fellowship is distinct from other kinds. Answers here should be restricted to characteristics of fellowship that *only* Christians can experience.

Point out, at this time, that neither this session nor chapter 2 of Philippians is an exhaustive study of Christian fellowship. Three essential characteristics are highlighted, as Dr. Wiersbe indicates.

Outlines are helpful for meaningful study. They help show relationships and also help in remembering what is studied. Use chalkboard 3 as an outline guide, adding other sub-ideas as you discuss them.

Ask, *In what ways does "in mind" indicate the extent and depth of fellowship?* (Whatever or whomever a person is most interested in, he naturally, and without effort, thinks about the most. You don't have to make yourself think about the things or people you really care about.) *How, or when, is considerable thought about a person* not *a sign of fellowship?* (When that person is feared, hated, or resented. Having such a person "in mind" reflects the very opposite of fellowship. In other words, *how* you have others in mind is every bit as important as *how much* you have them in mind.)

Ask several class members to read Philippians 1:3-6 from a number of different translations (make sure before class that three or four versions are available). *In light of verse 6, what is the source or essential ingredient of Christian fellowship?* (A right relationship to God; that is, God's having begun His work of salvation in us.) *What, then, is the source of* joyful *Christian fellowship?* (God continuing to work out His will in and through our lives. The degree to which we allow God to work in us not only determines the degree of effectiveness of our service but also determines the degree of satisfaction and joy we experience.)

What are the two basic kinds of friction that develop between believers? (The first kind is caused when one person is moving and the other is not; one is active and the other is idle and indifferent. The second kind is caused when both are moving, but in opposite or contrary directions. See *Text,* p. 30.) *What essential element of fellowship is lacking in both these situations?* (Commonness; in these instances, a lack of commonness of direction and purpose.) Friction, obviously, is incompatible with true fellowship.

How does love, which is evidence of our keeping others "in heart" as well as "in mind," affect friction and fellowship? (As the author suggests [p. 31], love acts as a lubricant to reduce friction between people. In so doing, it encourages fellowship, or at least protects it from deteriorating.) *Can love, even of the deepest sort, make up for lack of commonness?* (No; it can only keep down irritation and encourage the two parties to develop more commonness. Love, in itself, does not cure all problems. Nearly always, other ingredients—such as forgiveness, truthfulness, honesty, repentance—are absolutely necessary before a problem can be resolved. But love always makes problem-solving or resolving easier and less painful.)

In order to make this study as practical as possible, make sure that general principles are always well-illustrated. For instance, ask your adults for *specific* ways to show concern for others (see *Text,* pp. 31-32). Concern that never gets past the thought stage is not really concern. The ways it can be expressed are limitless, but the one absolute requirement is that

Chalkboard 2
See first paragraph under **Presentation.** The first list should pertain to all kinds of fellowship, the second list should include only those characteristics that are distinctly Christian.

```
FELLOWSHIP IS...



CHRISTIAN FELLOWSHIP IS...

2
```

it meet some need. Since we have different talents, gifts, and resources, the ways we are able to help others will vary a great deal. The concerned Christian does not presume to try to meet all of the needs of his fellow believers. But he uses what he *has* to do what he *can*.

Why is forgiveness one of the most difficult, yet one of the most significant, evidences of genuine love? (It is hard, because it runs contrary to our pride—which tempts us to resent and get even, or at least to keep a mental record of offenses against us. It is significant because nothing restores fellowship between Christians like genuine forgiveness. And love smoothes the way for forgiveness.)

After recounting the story (*Text,* p. 32) about the quiz contestant who could not remember his wife's blunders, ask, *Did this man's response indicate that he had a poor memory or that he was dishonest?* (It proved neither. His forgetting was an act of will, motivated by love. When his wife's blunders would come to mind, he determined not to dwell on them but to think of something else—until the thoughts of them no longer came to him. He did not deny that his wife had made blunders—which, of course, would have been dishonest—but he did deny, in effect, that he had a right to keep a record of them, and much less to tell others of them.)

As you discuss keeping other Christians "in prayer" (*Text,* pp. 32-35), you will again want to ask for specific suggestions concerning how and for what we should pray. *What is our most important consideration in prayer so far as the other Christian is concerned?* (His specific needs as we are able to know them.) *What is our most important consideration in prayer so far as God is concerned?* (His will and glory.) *Are these considerations ever incompatible?* (No. Since it is the Father's will to meet all the *real* needs of His children, and since He glorifies Himself by manifesting His love and grace in so doing, they could never be incompatible. One of the wonders of the Gospel is that God's best interest is always in our best interest.)

Assignment
Read chapter 3 of the text.

OUTLINE OF PHIL. 1:3-11

1:3-6 In my mind

1:7-8 In my heart

1:9-11 In my prayers

3

Chalkboard 3
You will want to add subheads to the outline depending on what subjects you discuss under each section.

SESSION 3

Pioneers Wanted / Text, Chapter 3

Session Goal
The purpose of this session should be to help class members understand how God often uses what seem to the world, and to us, as disadvantages to His and our advantage.

Preparation
As you prepare this lesson, remember that this study guide is meant to be just that—a guide, not a complete blueprint for you to follow slavishly. Occasionally, you may decide not to use the suggestions made here. Feel free. You will perhaps want to change the goals sometimes, because you feel other emphases in the text or Bible passage are more important or meaningful.

The important thing is that you *plan,* and plan carefully, for each session and for each part of the session. As this very lesson teaches, our plans should always be willingly subject to God's changing. But we should have some plans for Him to change, if necessary. To go into a classroom unprepared is not a sign of faith but of presumption.

Presentation
You may want to begin the session by developing the idea just mentioned under *Preparation.* Comment that God expects us to use our minds for Him. To think of ways we can serve the Lord more effectively is a sign of concern for His work. Paul had his own ideas about where he would go and what he would do. There is no hint in Scripture that God condemned or corrected him for making such plans, because He knew His servant's motives. A father is pleased and happy when his young son does something to "help" Daddy. The "help" is usually more of a hindrance, but the thoughtful parent certainly does not chastise the child for his efforts or ideas. He thanks the child for his concern and then shows him how the work really should be done. God did not rebuke Paul for planning to go to Bithynia; He simply redirected him to Macedonia (Acts 16:6-10). He did not accuse the apostle of presumption for wanting to go to Spain to preach the Gospel (Rom. 15:24); He simply sent him elsewhere.

Paul's intention was to go to Rome to preach the Gospel openly and publicly; instead he went there as a prisoner and was able to work only in confinement. *Was the apostle's basic purpose frustrated?* (No, because his purpose for preaching was to spread the Gospel, and this he was still able to do—even more effectively than he had planned; see *Text,* p. 37).

What is the essential characteristic of a pioneer? (Willingness to venture into the unknown and unproven.) *Can a "stay-at-home" be a pioneer?* (Yes; it has nothing necessarily to do with travel. Mrs. Spurgeon's ministry through the Book Fund extended to most of the British Isles, though she was confined to her own home; see *Text,* pp. 38-39).

Divide into three groups (or three sets of groups) to study the three unlikely "tools"—chains, critics, and crisis—that God often uses to accomplish His purposes. Assign each group one of the Scripture passages involved (see *Text*) and allow about 10 minutes to look for and discuss the various truths and principles involved in God's using these "tools" in His work. Each group should also review the relevant sections of the text.

After the class reassembles, the following questions may be useful in expanding on what the groups have to report (see chalkboard 4).

Chains (Phil. 1:12-14). According to verse 12, what was the primary work God used the apostle's "chains"—meaning all of his afflictions and frustrations and limitations—*to accomplish?* (The furtherance of the Gospel.) *What was one of the first practical means of this furtherance that Dr. Wiersbe mentions?* (Contact with many of the unsaved whom Paul would not otherwise have met or had opportunity to influence for Christ.)

How did Paul's "chains" aid in spreading the Gospel as far as other Christians were concerned? (His faithfulness and willingness to be used, without becoming bitter or resentful despite the worst of circumstances, gave encouragement to his fellow believers.)

What is the reverse side of the truth, illustrated by the blind man (Text, pp. 41-42), that adversity can become, in God's power, a great instrument for service? (The truth that prosperity, good health, and favorable circumstances often become, because of self-interest and self-satisfaction, means of sidetracking us from the Lord's work.)

Critics (Phil. 1:15-19). Was Paul oblivious to the faults and selfish motives of his opponents within the church? (No; in fact he specifically mentions their duplicity and spitefulness. The point of his comments in these verses was certainly not to justify these wicked men, but to teach two important truths: first, we should not let the shortcomings or criticisms of other Christians deter us or embitter us in the Lord's work;

	SATAN'S PURPOSE	GOD'S PURPOSE
CHAINS –	restrict Paul	spread Gospel
CRITICS –	discredit Paul	preach Gospel
CRISIS –	discourage Paul	magnify Christ

Chalkboard 4
Use this figure, or a similar one, to summarize graphically the group reports as they are given and discussed.

second, we should rejoice when, as often happens, God uses that which is intended for evil to accomplish His will.)

What truths does the story of Wesley and Whitefield (Text, p. 43) have for evangelicals today? (We can conscientiously and persistently disagree with another Christian's interpretation of Scripture without impugning his salvation or his sincerity. And even though we may not feel led to worship and serve in exactly the same ways, we should have love and respect for all true children of God and encourage them in every way we can and support them in prayer.)

Crisis (Phil. 1:20-26). How can what we say or do or endure "magnify" Christ? (Obviously, as Dr. Wiersbe points out, Christ cannot be made any greater than He already is. What is enlarged is His image, men's view of Him. It is man's assessment of Christ that is small and needs magnification. When He is shown to be what He is, man's view of Him is enlarged; see the text illustrations of the telescope and microscope.)

How does the statement, "Life is what we are alive to" (Text, p. 46), relate to God's using Paul's crisis to further the Gospel? (Paul was first of all concerned about, "alive to," spiritual, godly things. It was of little consequence to him, therefore, that his physical, earthly life and welfare were constantly threatened. Paul's real life was not diminished an iota by these seemingly unfortunate events; in fact, in and through all these he actually became more alive.)

If time permits, you may want to expand on the formula, "For to me to live is . . . , and to die is . . . ," mentioned in the text (see chalkboard 5).

Assignment
Read chapter 4 of the text.

Chalkboard 5
If you have time, you may want to pose the questions to your class that are given at the end of chapter 3 in the text.

FOR ME TO LIVE IS...
money | serve Lord
prestige |

FOR ME TO DIE IS...
leave all behind | be with Christ
be forgotten |

5

SESSION 4

Battle Stations / Text, Chapter 4

Session Goals
1. To consider what the Scripture text teaches about the relation of belief to practice; right doctrine to right living.
2. To consider some of the implications of the Christian's "spiritual warfare," especially as it pertains to defending the faith.
3. To study and discuss three essential elements—consistency, cooperation, and confidence—of faithful Christian service.

Preparation
Read chapter 4 of the text several times, making notes as usual, keeping in mind the three session goals suggested above. You may want to concentrate on one or two of these goals, depending on what you think the needs of your class are.

Presentation
This would be a good time to review briefly what has been studied so far, especially the emphases of sessions two and three—fellowship and furtherance. As Dr. Wiersbe points out in the opening paragraph of chapter 4, these two ideas are closely related to defending the faith, the focus of Philippians 1:27-30.

The term "faith," as used in Scripture, has several meanings. The most common is that of belief in, trusting, relying upon. This is the meaning used when we speak of saving faith. But "the faith of the Gospel" (Phil. 1:27) is almost a synonym for the Word of God. It refers especially to what may be called Gospel truth. The faith of the Gospel, then, is Christian doctrine.

Since there is so much emphasis today, inside and outside the Church, on spiritual experience, doctrine is often given short shrift. Some evangelicals come close to saying that what a Christian believes isn't important —so long as he is saved and tries to live a moral and helpful life. As the text clearly points out, however, how we live is determined directly, if not exclusively, by what we believe. For example, if we doubt that unbelievers are destined for hell, our reason for witnessing is eroded. In other words, *what* the Gospel teaches (1:27b) is the only means by which we can determine whether or not our lives conform to, are "becoming" to (1:27a), the Gospel.

Merely knowing what is right, of course, is never enough. Chapter 4 of *Be Joyful* highlights three essential requirements for faithful living once the right way is known.

A popular idea among many modern thinkers is that "consistency is the bugaboo of small minds." In other words, they maintain, the sophisticated person "in the know" recognizes that, since there are no absolutes, we shouldn't expect things, spiritual, moral, or other, to be consistent. This is the thinking behind what is usually called situation ethics: you must decide in the light of each particular situation what is right or wrong, good or harmful.

But according to Scripture, consistency in following God is the mark of a *great* person. When Christians live *in*consistently, they give "ammunition" to scoffers and unbelievers.

Why is consistency of life especially important as far as witnessing is concerned? (Because it gives evidence to others that we take the Gospel seriously and that the Gospel not only brings new life but a new way of living; see *Text,* pp. 51-52.)

Does Paul's counsel that Christians should not be frightened by their opponents (1:28) mean that these opponents cannot do believers any harm? (No; in fact he goes on in the next verse to speak of the suffering they will often cause Christians. It is obviously of spiritual harm and of the final outcome that we are not to be afraid.)

In what ways are John 16:33 and 2 Timothy 3:12, which Dr. Wiersbe mentions (p. 55), *negative promises of God?* (They are just as much His conditional promises as are the Beatitudes, only they stress the cost, rather than the blessings, of discipleship. It is in spite of, and even because of, these afflictions that Christians are to have confidence. See chalkboard 6.)

What blessings or encouragements does a Christian have because of his adversities suffered for Christ's sake? (Adversities are evidence that he is saved [v. 28], they are a gift and an honor from the Lord in that we are privileged to suffer for His sake [v. 29], they place us in the unique fellowship of spiritual giants who have also suffered for Him [see v. 30], and they are a means of spiritual maturity and strengthening.)

Assignment
Read chapter 5 of the text.

Chalkboard 6
All of God's promises, when the necessary conditions are met, lead to the victorious, joyful life.

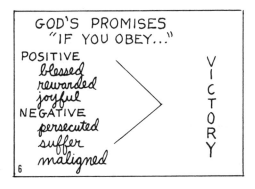

15

SESSION 5

The Great Example / Text, Chapter 5

Session Goals
1. To understand better what the submissive mind is, looking at Christ as the supreme Example.
2. To discover ways we may individually grow in submissiveness.

Preparation
Since, as mentioned previously, *Be Joyful* is not an exhaustive study of Philippians, much less of each doctrine or truth it teaches, many questions are likely to be raised in class that are not dealt with in the text. Such is the case with the present session. The key emphasis is humility, or the submissive mind, and the key illustration is the earthly life of the Lord Jesus Christ. Pride, sacrifice, and glorifying God are also discussed. So you will need to be careful not to get sidetracked into dealing with any of these themes in detail, as important as they are.

The theme of Philippians 2 and of chapters 5—7 of the text is "others." Chapters 5 and 7 focus on examples of serving others—first Jesus, then Timothy and Epaphroditus. Chapter 6 is a more general approach.

More than usual, perhaps, this session pertains almost exclusively to Christians. Depending on the makeup of your class, you may need to make it clear that, before Jesus can be our example, He must first be our Saviour and Lord.

Presentation
Begin by asking, *Why does selfishness never bring joy?* (Refer to the Augustine quote mentioned under session 1 of this guide. We were not made to serve ourselves—or anything or anyone other than God. The self-centered life is therefore misdirected and off balance, and cannot be fulfilling and satisfying.)

Using chalkboard 7, discuss briefly some of the things humility is and is not. As with meekness, love, and many other concepts, a lot of people —including some Christians—have ideas about humility that are far from biblical. Ask for characteristics of humility. After each suggestion, let the class determine—in light of Scripture and the text—whether the suggestion should be listed under "is" or under "is not."

You may want to ask, during this activity, *Why is humility not a matter of running down or degrading ourselves?* (Jesus taught that we are to love ourselves [Mark 12:33]. Besides, it would be dishonest to claim, for instance, that we are less talented or blessed than we really are.) *How does this square, then, with Paul's claim that he was chief of sinners?* (Paul was speaking of himself *in* himself. In ourselves, of course, we are *all* completely sinful and absolutely unworthy of God's grace, love, or blessings. Paul also readily acknowledged that he was a child of God and an apostle and that the Lord had done many wonderful things in and through him. Humility does not discount the good in our lives; but it is careful to give all the credit for it to God.)

Does humility, or submissiveness to others, mean doing everything they want us to do? (Hardly. God's virtues are never inconsistent with one another. Being humble, therefore, could never cause one to do anything sinful. Besides, it is never for another person's good to do anything that is sinful, no matter how much he may desire it.)

Does "not thinking of ourselves" (Text, pp. 58-59) mean that we never take ourselves into consideration? (No. We could hardly love ourselves or take the beam out of our own eye—to name but a few scriptural commands—unless we took ourselves into account. The idea is that we put the interests and welfare of others above our own. Our "selves" are not to be at the center of our thinking and concerns.)

What does "the mind of Christ" (Phil. 2:5-8) teach us about demanding our "rights"? (In the first place, most of the concepts of human rights are more worldly than biblical. But even rights that truly belong to us, we must be willing to surrender for the sake of our Lord and of others, following His great example. If He gave up His absolute rights and privileges for us, how much more should we be willing to give up our very limited and undeserved rights.)

Why is pride the great enemy not only of humility but of the spiritual life in general? (It is the basis of all other sin. It is the supreme idolatry, because it puts self in God's place; it dethrones God. See Text, pp. 60-61; chalkboard 8.)

Have Matthew 20:28 read from several translations. *Judging from this verse, how is Jesus our supreme example?* (We, like Him, are to shun being served and to seek opportunities to serve others.) *How, judging from this same verse, is He very much* not *our example?* (We cannot even redeem ourselves, much less any others—no matter how much we might sacrifice.)

In what way is Jesus' cross-bearing a model for our own? (It is self-

Chalkboard 7
Your class members may not agree as to the classification of a given suggestion under "is" or "is not." As far as possible, let Scripture be your arbiter.

HUMILITY IS	HUMILITY IS NOT
acknowledging our limitations	denying talent
giving God credit and glory	running ourselves down

7

accepted but not self-inflicted. Jesus was not punishing Himself, but willingly accepting punishment from others. Cross-bearing is not making things hard on ourselves, as many in the Middles Ages did in order to gain some merit with God.) *In what way is cross-bearing different from all other types of suffering?* (It is only that suffering which comes to us because of our faithfulness to God. No matter how obedient to the Lord we may be, suffering or persecution is not a cross unless it comes to us *because of* our faithfulness.)

In what way is glorifying God (Text, p. 66) *much like magnifying Him* (See session 3)? (We cannot add anything, whether greatness or glory, to God. But a faithful, obedient, loving Christian makes God's greatness and glory more evident to others.)

What are the only two right motives for wanting others to see our good works? (First, that these works might bring glory to God [Matt. 5:16], and, second, that they might be an encouragement and example to other believers; see *Text,* p. 67.)

Assignment
Read chapter 6 of the text.

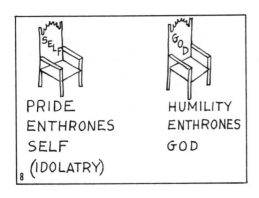

Chalkboard 8
Use this simple drawing to illustrate how pride is a form of idolatry.

SESSION 6

The Ins and Outs of Christian Living / Text, Chapter 6

Session Goals
1. To discover how to go from biblical precept to daily practice.
2. To discuss some of the problems and potentials of the Christian life that is single-minded and submissive.

Preparation
Since there is a great deal of "meat" in this chapter of the text, it will be easier than usual to get sidetracked or to spend so long on the earlier parts that you run out of time before you are half through the material. It would probably be advisable to put an outline on the board (chalkboard 9) for both you and the class to follow. An outline also helps you see continuity and relationships.

Presentation
Have someone read Philippians 2:1-18 and then briefly review the highlights of session 5, which was based on verses 1-11. Ask, *Why, as Dr. Wiersbe suggests, is the true Christian life more incarnation than imitation?* (Because it is first of all Christ living in and through us, not our patterning our lives after His. As discussed last session, God does not expect His children to be able to follow Christ's example in their own power, any more than He expected them to be saved in their own power.) *What is necessary, on our part, for both salvation and spiritual living?* (Faith, trusting God to do for us what we cannot do for ourselves.)

Of the three illustrations—mathematics, mining, and farming—given in the text, which do you think best illustrates "working out our own salvation"? (Probably mining. It represents great wealth, which the miner or owner had nothing to do with creating. Mining, or working out the ore contributes nothing to its intrinsic value but is essential in order for the wealth to be appropriated. All the gold, or whatever, belongs to the owner even before any of it is mined but he cannot really take advantage of it until it is worked out.)

Ask the class to suggest some paraphrases for "work out your own salvation." (Possible suggestions might be: Work out God's plan in your daily living; let God complete the work through you that He began in you at conversion.)

What does Philippians 2:15 suggest about the relationship between circumstances and faithfulness? (There is none. It is possible to live the ideal Christian life in the least ideal circumstances. Since the Fall, circumstances have *never* been conducive to godly living.)

You may want to say a few words, as you begin the second section of the lesson ("a power to receive"), about the relationship of God's provision and His commands. Explain briefly how God delivered, led, provided for, and encouraged the Israelites long *before* He gave them the Ten Commandments. And He continued to lead, protect, provide, and encourage *after* the commandments were given. Here we see clearly the dominant biblical principle that God's provision, His energizing, both precedes and follows His commands. At no time has God expected men to do *His* will in their *own* power.)

Is God's power the only energy that is available to men? (No; we have energy within ourselves to accomplish certain things, and this is the energy of the flesh [Rom. 7:5]. The devil is ready to provide us with energy as well [Eph. 2:2; 2 Thes. 2:7].) *What kind of work, however, are neither of these kinds of energy able to accomplish?* (God's work, anything that is spiritually worthwhile.)

Why do you suppose Dr. Wiersbe calls God's Word, prayer, and suffering "tools" of the Holy Spirit? (None of these, not even the Word, have power in themselves to accomplish God's purposes. They are channels which must be empowered by His Holy Spirit in order to be effective.)

Write *appreciate, appropriate,* and *apply* in one column on the board (see chalkboard 10) and, to the right, list *life, mind,* and *heart.* Ask, *To which word on the right does each word on the left correspond?* Draw lines as answers are given.

What effect does suffering, or any type of affliction, usually have on the natural or carnal Christian mind? (It generally causes bitterness, resentment, and hardness of heart.) *What effect does it have on the spiritual mind, the one that is single and submissive?* (It makes it more humble, and softens the heart; see *Text,* p. 76)

Unless he had died or moved away, the jailer who was converted through Paul's witness (Acts 16:25-34) must have belonged to the church at Philippi. *What do you suppose he thought about Paul's admonition in 2:15?* (A speculation, of course, but it was likely one of the jailer's favorite passages in this letter to his home church, for he had seen the apostle

PHIL. 2:12-18
1. A Purpose to achieve (12, 14-16)
2. A Power to receive (13)
   TOOLS { God's Word
          { Prayer
          { Suffering
3. A Promise to believe (16-18)

Chalkboard 9
Add additional points to the outline as necessary, as you proceed through the lesson.

exemplify this very spirit [meekness] in this very type of situation [unjust affliction]. It was also this spirit that saved the jailer from suicide and made him receptive to the Gospel.)

In what sense does God "need" Christians in order to fully accomplish His work? (In the sense that electricity needs a conductor in order to flow and accomplish work. No intrinsic power is in the conduit, but it is the channel through which the current flows [see chalkboard 11]. God could use any means He might choose to work through—just as He could have raised up children to Abraham from stones [Matt. 3:9]—but He has chosen Christians to be His primary channels of witness and work.)

Based on the themes of these last two sessions (5 and 6), *how might we express God's "formula" for spiritual success and joy?* (Christ's example plus the Spirit's energy [with our submissiveness as catalyst] equals joyful success. See *Text,* last sentence of chap. 6.)

Assignment

Ask for volunteers for the research and report project for next session. Read chapter 7 in the text.

Chalkboard 10
Use this diagram as a simple matching test. Write the six words on the board as shown and ask members to cross-match them.

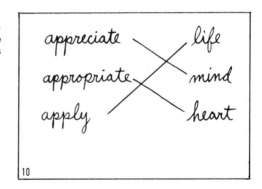

Chalkboard 11
To illustrate Dr. Wiersbe's comment about electricity needing a conductor, use this figure. Draw the generator and light bulb first, then the two wires as the essential conductor between them.

SESSION 7

A Priceless Pair / Text, Chapter 7

Session Goals
To help students gain insight and encouragement from two outstanding examples of the submissive mind.

Preparation
Study the text carefully, looking up and making notes on all Scripture passages listed. Here would be a good opportunity to involve class members in the session. Ask two students to research and report on the two subjects of this lesson—Timothy and Epaphroditus. Their best resources will be Bible dictionaries or encyclopedias. Assign the projects at least a week in advance.

Presentation
In the minds of most Christians, not only Christ and Paul but also Timothy and Epaphroditus are in "another league" from us spiritually. You will probably do well, therefore, to spend time emphasizing that God has but one standard for all of His children—perfection (Matt. 5: 48). His spiritual gifts, callings, and blessings vary from Christian to Christian, but His doctrinal and moral standards are uniform. So are His expectations of obedience. *All* of Christ's disciples are to be single-minded and totally submissive.

Review the illustrations of indifference with which chapter 7 opens, adding, if possible, a more recent incident that would be familiar to your class. Ask, *What are some of the more understandable excuses people give for not helping others?* (Fear of being sued; fear that they will have to testify as a witness in a long court case; fear that they may do the wrong thing, such as move an injured person who should be kept still.) *Why, however, do even such "reasonable" excuses really not excuse us?* (We are commanded by God to aid others who are in trouble. Inconvenience, risk of legal suit, and perhaps even physical danger, are often the costs of being a Good Samaritan. No-risk help is a sub-Christian standard of neighborliness.) *What are often the* real *reasons we fail to help when we can?* (Indifference, cold-heartedness, self-concern—which are *not* small sins.)

At this time ask for the report on Timothy. (Allow about five minutes.) You will want to adapt and add to the following questions, in accordance with the ideas and insights reported.

What definite advantage did Timothy have at the time of his conversion? (Both his mother and grandmother were Christians.) *What additional great advantage did he come to have a few years later?* (The opportunity to work and travel with the great Apostle Paul.)

Is a "servant's mind" a natural attribute? (If, by "natural," we mean a trait that is characteristic of man's fallen nature, the answer is no, although some unsaved persons do have an inclination and ability to help others that is far above the average.) You should point out that Dr. Wiersbe uses "natural" in two different senses in the section on Timothy. In the paragraph beginning, "In Timothy's experience" (*Text,* p. 81), he says that it was not natural for Timothy to be a servant. Here the idea is that, before his conversion and perhaps immediately after it, he was probably not known for his helpfulness. In the next two paragraphs, the author speaks of Timothy's "natural" concern for others. Here, apparently, the meaning is that, as his gift of serving was developed, Timothy's concern for others became more and more characteristic of him.

Several of the spiritual gifts—such as pastoring and hospitality—involve direct service or helpfulness to others. Is the fact that many Christians do not have these particular gifts any excuse for their not having a "servant's mind"? (No, the Lord calls all His followers to be servants, to be self-giving, concerned for others' welfare above their own.)

Why is training essential to being a good servant? (Good intentions and motives are never enough for effectiveness in anything. As mentioned in regard to helping victims of an accident, ignorance of sound first-aid procedure could lead the best-intentioned person to kill or seriously cripple the very person he tries to help. A Christian cannot be spiritually helpful without being spiritually informed.)

Dr. Wiersbe has an excellent illustration of this truth (the popular entertainer who was converted and immediately wanted to be a "big name for Christ"). *What two very serious mistakes did this man make?* (First, he assumed that the power of the Gospel and of the Holy Spirit would be enhanced by his own worldly popularity and influence. Second, he assumed that his mere conversion qualified him as a spiritual leader.) *What basic sin was behind both these assumptions?* (Pride; in many ways, he himself—rather than the Lord—was still the center of his concern and confidence.) This man's philosophy of Christian witness and service is all too common in evangelical circles today. But worldly means can never serve spiritual ends.

In addition to the heavenly reward he would receive, how was Timothy also rewarded and blessed on earth? (Perhaps most outstandingly by being chosen to carry on much of Paul's ministry. Because he had been faithful in a few responsibilities, he was given mastery over many others.)

After the report on Epaphroditus has been given, use the following questions as guides for discussion:

What words does Paul use, in describing Epaphroditus (Phil. 2:25), *that indicate the latter's personableness and friendliness?* (Brother, companion, and fellow soldier.) *What words, in this same verse, indicate that Epaphroditus' friendship was not passive, or in words only?* (He was a brother and companion in *labor,* he was a fellow *soldier,* he was a *messenger,* and he *ministered.* He was obviously no mere fair-weather friend.)

You may want to add the rather well-known observation that Christianity, for many believers, is much like a football game. In the stands are thousands of spectators desperately in need of exercise watching 22 men on the field who are desperately in need of rest. Paul, Timothy, and Epaphroditus were far from being spectator Christians.

Is it wrong or worldly to give reasonable recognition and esteem to God's servants who serve Him selflessly and effectively? (No; in fact it is scriptural to do so [1 Thes. 5:12-13].) *What, however, is the key word in the previous question that makes an important qualification to this principle?* ("Reasonable," which means, in the first place, that all glory and basic honor is given to God. We also need to take care lest well-intended praise be a cause for our brother's stumbling in pride.)

Assignment
Read chapter 8 in the text.

SESSION **8**

Learning How to Count / Text, Chapter 8

Session Goals
1. To consider in depth the differences between works righteousness and faith righteousness.
2. To consider why the one is futile and the other effective as the means of salvation.

Preparation
As you prepare this lesson, "audit" your own life to find areas in which you may still be trusting in some sort of works instead of entirely in Christ. We can no more complete or perfect our salvation by anything we do than we could have been saved by self-effort or doing good. The unsaved person is not the only one who is tempted to trust in works righteousness.

Presentation
Both works righteousness and faith righteousness are based on faith. The difference is in what, or who, is trusted. In works righteousness, a man trusts (has faith in) himself, in what he can do for God. In what is often called faith righteousness, a man trusts in what God, through Christ, has done for him. (See chalkboard 12.) Both of these systems involve works, too. The first relies on man's works, the second on God's work.

Review, briefly, the account of Acts 15:1-29, using related comments from the text. The philosophy began early in the life of the Church, and continuing in various forms and degrees for many years, that a Gentile must become a Jew if he were to be a Christian. The strongest proponents of this heresy, as might be expected, were Pharisees (v. 5). These men were believers (see also v. 5) but wanted to add to the Gospel of Christ. Their additions were not exactly man-made. They were standards that God Himself had given to His chosen people, the Jews—namely, the rite of circumcision and the Law of Moses.

Circumcision and the Law were not wrong in themselves. Far from it. The mistake lay in taking something that was God-ordained and using it in a way and for a purpose that God did not intend. As is often observed, the worst things are frequently the best things corrupted or misused. Even under the Old Covenant, God had never intended either circumcision or obedience to the Law to be in any sense the means of salvation. As Romans 4:1-8 and many other passages make clear, faith in God has *always* been the *only* means of salvation.

Before the Jerusalem Council (Acts 15), many of the Judaizers, or legalists, were no doubt perfectly sincere and innocent of any wrong motivation. But after this time when the Gospel was clarified in relation to these false concepts, the ones who still held to them were consciously and intentionally opposing the Gospel. They were plainly heretics, and Paul gave them no excuse or justification (Phil. 3:2).

As you discuss confidence in the flesh—the primary sin of which the Judaizers were guilty—you may want to recount the illustration from the last session (*Text,* pp. 82-83) about the converted entertainer. His purpose was right—to serve the Lord—but his means were worldly, fleshly. He wanted to use the same means to serve the Lord that he had been using to serve the world—after he had "baptized" them and cleaned them up a bit. The Judaizers wanted to continue serving God in the flesh under the New Covenant just as they had done under the Old.

In what way is the rowboat an inappropriate figure (*Text,* p. 94) *to illustrate the means of salvation?* (Though one oar is called *faith* and the other *works,* both are powered by the man rowing. "Faith" is simply a disguise for another form of self-effort. There is no place for God in the illustration.)

Read Galatians 6:12-13. *Why were many of the Judaizers attracted to works righteousness, exemplified in circumcision?* (To "make a good show in the flesh." The world has always admired self-effort, religious or other, and looks up to the self-sufficient.) *What was, perhaps, their negative motivation along this same line?* (They compromised the Gospel to avoid persecution. Paul, however—as all the faithful Christians of his time— was uncompromising in spite of persecution; see *Text,* p. 95.)

Why is sincerity, as important as it is, never sufficient by itself? (Like faith, it is only as secure and reliable as its object. If *what* is believed is wrong, the strength of the belief itself only compounds and entrenches the falsehood. The *more* sincere a person is, the *worse* off he is, if what he is sincere about is mistaken. The more sincerely a person holds on to falsehood, the more he resists accepting the truth.)

Did all the things Paul counted as refuse or garbage (Phil. 3:5-6) *have the same value or worth in themselves?* (Not at all. The first list [v. 5] included things that were completely acceptable in themselves. Some were even commanded by God. The other list [v. 6], includes persecuting

Chalkboard 12
Draw the two figures as shown as you discuss the truth that faith is only as strong as that in which it is placed. Only Christ is able either to save or to support us.

the Church, which of course was completely wrong, despite his sincerity about it.) *In what way only were these things all considered as garbage?* (As means of salvation or of earning any merit or righteousness before God. See *Text,* pp. 97-98.)

When discussing the second point under "Paul's gains" (*Text,* p. 98), have the class read Romans 4:1-8, as Dr. Wiersbe suggests. *How many times is the idea of being counted righteous mentioned in these eight verses?* (Six, since the term *justification* means this very thing.) *What is the opposite side* (vv. 7-8) *of this same truth?* (A believer's sins are *not* counted.)

Assignment
Read chapter 9 in the text.

SESSION 9

Let's Win the Race! / Text, Chapter 9

Session Goals
To learn better what it means to be a "winning Christian" and to fulfill the purposes for which we have been saved.

Preparation
One of the persistent threats to the spiritual health of the Church has been the unbiblical idea frequently called "only believism." Few people admit to holding this philosophy, but many live as if they believed it. Basically, it is the concept that all God expects of a man is that he trust in Christ for salvation. It tends to look on obedience to New Testament commands as a form of legalism, or at best an "extra" which is not really binding on Christians. In short, "only believism" looks on the new birth as both the beginning and end of the Christian experience.

"Only believism" is somewhat the opposite of "works righteousness," which overemphasizes man's part. It falsely and illogically concludes that, since man cannot earn salvation by works, he has no work to do after salvation, either. The New Testament contradicts this philosophy from beginning to end. We are not saved *by* good works, but we certainly are saved in order to *produce* good works (Eph. 2:10; 1 Cor. 15:58). "Winning the race" is one of the many figures the New Testament uses to signify our fulfilling the work Christ has for us to do on earth.

As you plan this session, decide—according to the needs of your class—how much emphasis and time you will devote to each of the five essentials discussed for winning this race.

Presentation
Summarize the last paragraph before the heading "Dissatisfaction" (*Text*, p.105) as a sort of introduction to this study.

1. *Dissatisfaction (Phil. 3:12-13a).* Why do you suppose the author claims that "a sanctified dissatisfaction is the first essential to progress in the Christian race"? (A person who is satisfied with himself—what he is like, what he is doing, etc.—is not inclined to move at all, much less to race. There is a great deal of difference in being satisfied with what Christ has done for us and being satisfied with what we are doing for Him.)

Why do many Christians, like many non-Christians, seem pretty well pleased with their moral and spiritual lives? (Because they measure themselves by human, not divine, standards—and sometimes not by very high human standards.) *What is God's one and only standard for all believers?* (Jesus Christ; in other words, perfection. Use chalkboard 13 as you discuss these two questions.)

It is often observed that the truly informed and intelligent person is one who realizes how much he doesn't know yet. This principle also applies to the truly spiritual person. The more he grows in the Lord, the clearer view he has of the Lord and the more he realizes he still falls far short of the Lord.

In relation to the two extremes of self-evaluation (*Text,* pp. 106-107), ask, *What do the errors of bragging and running ourselves down have in common?* (Focus on self rather than Christ. Both are self-centered.)

2. *Devotion (3:13a).* This virtue is obviously an aspect of spiritual single-mindedness. *To what special area of our lives does this particular type of singleness pertain?* (To our work for the Lord, concentration and specialization in the particular calling He has for us. It includes not being sidetracked or having our energy dissipated by trying to be Christian "jacks of all trades." Obviously some believers are more gifted and have more diversified callings than do others, but no Christian is given every gift and called to be active in every type of Christian endeavor [see 1 Cor. 12:4-5, 29-30; etc.]. See chalkboard 14.)

3. *Direction (3:13b). What does the Bible mean by God's, and our own, "forgetfulness" of sins that have been forgiven by Christ?* (It means that these sins should no longer be taken into consideration, that they should be treated as if they had never been committed; see *Text,* pp. 108-109.) *Why, in this sense, is a "poor memory" an asset to effective and efficient Christian work?* (Our past sins and failures do not distract our attention and sap our energy from the work we are presently doing for the Lord. We are able to learn and profit from past mistakes without being haunted by them.)

A good runner never looks back. Even a relay runner doesn't look back for the baton; he trusts the other runner to put it in his hand at the right time. Looking back, for whatever reason, breaks your stride and slows you down. It may even make you get out of your lane and so be disqualified altogether. *What is the only direction a racer, including a spiritual racer, should be concerned about?* (Forward, the direction of the goal.)

4. *Determination (3:14). What are the two extremes to avoid in considering God's and man's part in doing His work?* (Expecting God to do

Chalkboard 13
Men are satisfied with their character and achievements simply because they are satisfied with human standards.

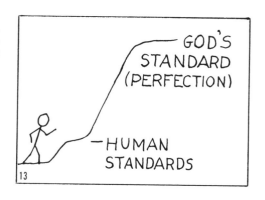

it all and expecting man to do it all. All the power, of course, is God's, through His Holy Spirit. But Scripture plainly teaches that there are certain things—many of them—that God expects *us* to do *in* His power.)

In what way does the winner of a physical race (see 1 Cor. 9:24) *not completely illustrate spiritual winning?* (In the Christian "race" each runner competes, as it were, against himself. *Every* Christian, therefore, can win.)

5. *Discipline (3:15-16)*. You may already have adequately covered this aspect of "winning" as you dealt with "only believism." The Christian life *does* have standards, higher ones than any given under the Old Covenant (see Matt. 5:21-48). We live the Christian life not only by God's Spirit but by His standards, His "rules."

Assignment
Read chapter 10 of the text carefully, noting the characteristics of spiritual mindedness and taking a personal inventory of your own life in light of these characteristics.

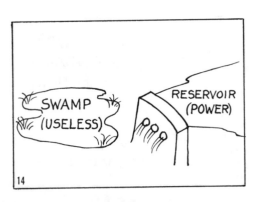

Chalkboard 14
To illustrate Dr. Wiersbe's comments about a river becoming a swamp or a reservoir, use this diagram.

SESSION 10

Living in the Future Tense / Text, Chapter 10

Session Goals
1. To understand spiritual mindedness: what it is and is not, what it does and does not do.
2. To discover ways of developing our own spiritual mindedness.

Preparation
Study chapter 10 of the text carefully, noting which parts you think will be of greatest concern and importance to your students. Plan to discuss, early in the class period, the different meanings of *spiritual*. When the term is unqualified in Scripture, it always has the positive meaning of godly, righteous, holy, and the like. Sometimes it is used in a more or less neutral theological or moral sense, as when it simply distinguishes the physical from the spiritual realms. All of the spiritual realm of course, is not good or godly. Satan is a spiritual being, as are all of his angels.

These distinctions should be obvious to your students, but a word of clarification—and of warning—may be in order if you think any of them might be confused by the teachings of certain popular modern sects, such as Christian Science, which holds that sin, evil, pain, illness, and the like are not realities at all, but purely imaginary. The Early Church was plagued by similar teachings. Gnosticism, a type of Greek philosophy that was quite influential in New Testament times, held that all the spiritual realm was good as such and all the physical was evil as such. This idea is obviously unscriptural and leads to many sorts of other false ideas—such as the belief that, since the body is physical and therefore entirely evil, it doesn't make any difference what you do to it or how you use it.

A common problem today is the tremendous influence of various types of mysticism, ESP, and the occult. Many people, including some undiscerning Christians, have been led to believe that some forms of these ideas and activities are perfectly safe, and even helpful—as long as they don't teach anything specifically immoral or denounce God. If something "works," they reason, it's bound to be good, especially if it is supernatural, and most especially if it is miraculous. Satan, of course, is both a supernatural and a miracle-working being. Pragmatism is no test for distinguishing good from evil, or right spirits from wrongs ones.

Presentation
After summarizing the comments under "Preparation," and adding others that you feel are necessary or helpful, ask, *Is spiritual mindedness a matter of knowledge or a matter of perspective?* (It is both. A spiritual person must be informed about basic biblical truths or he will have no

means of distinguishing truth from error, right from wrong. But he must also have the right perspective, the right orientation. Satan *knows* more spiritual truths than perhaps any Christian could ever know. But he rejects and hates God's truth. He sees it entirely through the "lenses" of his corrupt, rebellious, evil nature.)

You may want to add the illustration that a farmer on his tractor and a pilot flying at 5,000 feet may be looking at the same field—but what they see is vastly different (see chalkboard 15). Heavenly or spiritual mindedness does not pertain so much to *what* we see as to *how* we see it (see *Text,* p. 116).

In what sense is the expression, "Some Christians are so heavenly minded that they are of no earthly good" (*Text,* p. 116), *true and in what sense is it not?* (It is true only as "heavenly mindedness" is spurious or superficial. "Religious minded" would be much more accurate. The truly heavenly or spiritually minded person is of the greatest possible earthly good. He is exactly what the world needs. Jesus was perfectly heavenly minded and perfectly beneficial to earth. Our present heavenly task is to do God's work on earth.)

What is the two-fold (positive and negative) purpose of both good laws and good fences? (To protect as well as to restrict. In fact, even the restriction is primarily for our own good, as well as for the good of others. Obeying "heaven's laws" [*Text,* pp. 119-120] is really the highest form of self-interest. All of God's laws are for our best good as well as for His greatest glory; see chalkboard 16.)

Another false concept (see "Preparation") of spiritual mindedness is that it is a naïve, "see no evil" view of life that tends to ignore or discount truths that are unpleasant and hard. *Why was Paul (Phil. 3:18-19) led to weep about certain persons who were influencing, or trying to influence the Philippian church?* (They were enemies of the cross of Christ and were doomed to destruction if they did not repent. The Bible is just as explicit about the terror of being lost as it is about the wonder of being saved.)

In relation to being discouraged *(Text,* p. 122), tell about the incident in Luther's life when, as he was complaining to his wife how bad things were, she said, "Is God dead?" After his startled, "What do you mean?"

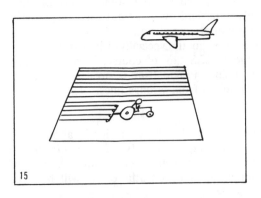

Chalkboard 15
To illustrate the difference that perspective makes, draw a field—at which both a farmer on his tractor and pilot in his plane are looking.

she commented, "Only if God were dead would you have a right to be so despondent."

Why is having the right priorities almost as important as having the right values? (We may believe all the right things and be doing all the wrongs things, but have them out of proportion. We may spend most of our time trying to figure out the meaning of obscure and secondary scriptural truths and give little attention to understanding and following the plain and important ones; see chalkboard 17.)

Assignment

While reading chapter 11, honestly appraise your own life to see if you are worried many times when you ought to be calm.

Chalkboard 16
Draw a simple fence, as indicated, and several figures inside to represent sheep. A wolf is outside. The fence keeps the sheep from wandering **and** from being attacked by the wolf.

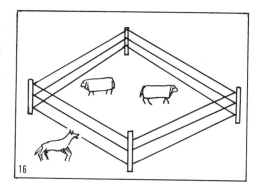

Chalkboard 17
Draw the top row of blocks to illustrate right values in a wrong order of priority. The second line represents right values in right order.

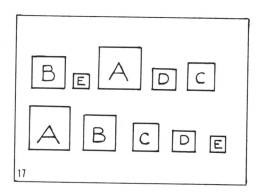

SESSION 11

You Don't Have to Worry! | *Text, Chapter 11*

Session Goals
1. To discover, from Philippians 4:1-9, some more (see session 1) causes of worry, some spiritual thieves of joy.
2. To discover God's plan for overcoming worry and for bringing peace, the secure mind.

Preparation
If your class is about average, many of your students will not think this session particularly relevant to them. They may find it interesting but apply most of the truths to other people. We do not have to be psychologists, just honest and thoughtful, to realize that we probably are much more anxious or worried or bothered—whatever term we might want to use—than we seem. Because it is so subtle and because it is a respectable vice—compared to most others—worry often goes undetected or at least unacknowledged. Like people who suspect they have a serious disease, we don't want to face up to the presence and seriousness of the problem sometimes until a great deal of damage—some of it permanent—has been done.

Two excellent resource books for this session are *How to Win over Worry*, by John Haggai, and *None of These Diseases*, by S. I. McMillen (may be secured at most Christian bookstores). Chapter 16, "David and the Giant—Worry," is particularly appropriate in McMillen's book.

Presentation
Review briefly the section on worry in chapter 1 of the text. *How much is worry related to the problems one is worried about?* (Very little. Paul's problems, when he wrote the epistle we are studying, were extremely serious but he was virtually free of worry. Refer also to the report given later in this chapter of the text that indicates that 92% of worries are groundless and unnecessary; p. 129.)

From the root meaning of the word translated "anxious" in 4:6 (see comments in *Text*, pp. 125-126), *what bearing does singlemindedness have on worry?* (A very direct bearing. Uncertainty is an integral part of worry. A person who is unsure of his standards and objectives is uncertain and is "pulled in different directions"; see chalkboard 18.)

In praying, which is more important, immensity or intensity? (The latter. Jesus explicitly said that we are not heard simply for "much praying" [Matt. 6:7b].)

The laser is one of the most remarkable and usable discoveries of modern science; yet its basic nature is extremely simple. It is nothing but highly integrated and intensified light. Part of its great value lies in the fact that so much can be done with so little. The finer the beam, the greater its value—especially in such uses as eye surgery. Its value is not the quantity of light it produces but the intensity. For all practical purposes, it has no diffusion, no stray light. Every ray is going in precisely the same direction.

Which is more important, right thinking or right doing? (Both are essential to right living, of course, but right thinking must always be involved. No truly right act has ever come from anything but a right thought. As a man thinks in his heart, so is he [Prov. 23:7].)

The most influential book in the most populated country in the world (China) is significantly called *The Thoughts of Chairman Mao,* and the influence of these thoughts reaches far beyond the borders of China. Acceptance of the basic ideas, the thoughts, in this little book is absolutely essential to keeping the people in subjection to communism. If the people should stop thinking like communists, they would stop acting like communists. When believers truly think like Christ, they act like Him.

The devil is a great thought-controller *(Text,* pp. 129-130). *But is it necessary to believe in Satan—that is, believe that he exists—in order to serve him?* (No, unlike God, he can easily be served even by those who deny him. Since everything apart from God is evil, everything apart from God serves Satan—regardless of the intentions of whoever does it.)

If time permits, you may want to do a comparative study of Philippians 4 and James 4, expanding on the ideas given in the text (pp. 131-132). Use the chalkboard and make parallel lists of positive (from Phil.) and negative (from James) principles of praying, thinking, and living. One set of principles produces war (including, sometimes, the literal kind), while the other set produces peace (see chalkboard 19).

Is worry a sin or merely a spiritual shortcoming? (It is clearly a sin. It is contrary to God's will for us and specifically breaks one of Jesus' commandments [Matt. 6:24-34].)

Which of the three aspects of prayer discussed in chapter 11 of the text (pp. 126-127) *is the best cure for worry or apprehension?* (Appreciation.) *Why?* (An opinion question, largely, but probably because it takes

Chalkboard 18
Draw the four horses, to which the man is tied, to illustrate this well-known form of torture. Men may also be torn apart inwardly by being pulled in different directions.

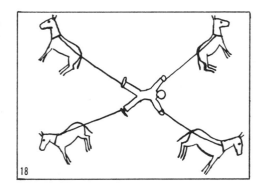

attention off ourselves and places it on God, and changes our focus from our problems to our blessings.)

Assignment

Read *Text,* chapter 12. Bring to class any questions you would like discussed further in the Review Session.

Chalkboard 19
Use a scheme such as this if you plan to do a comparison of Philippians and James as suggested under "Presentation."

PRINCIPLES OF PRAYING, THINKING, LIVING	
PHILIPPIANS (POSITIVE)	JAMES (NEGATIVE)

SESSION 12

The Secret of Contentment / Text, Chapter 12

Session Goals
To discover three of the basic spiritual resources of Christian contentment and joy, and to learn how better to rely upon God to provide all our needs.

Preparation
In some respects, chapter 12, like the Bible text on which it is based, is a summary of the epistle. Its major themes of God's providence, power, and promises have all been considered earlier. Since this is the case, you may want to cover the suggested material for this session in about half the period and then devote the rest of the time to sharing and mutual encouragement relating to each person's submitting to God wholly and experiencing more of the contentment and joy about which you have been studying. These truths, like all of God's truth, are not simply for us to know about and acknowledge but to profit from.

It is one of the most persistent tendencies of human nature for us to want to conform to those around us. Someone has pictured the relationship of many Christians to the world in a graphic way. These Christians are careful to hold themselves above the world's standards. But, as the world lowers its standards, so do they—though keeping the distance of separation. They feel perfectly "spiritual" as long as this separation is maintained. But what is their problem? The world is really their standard, not Christ. If Christ were their standard, then, the worse the world became, the greater the distance of separation. The secret of contentment is not to be somewhat better than the world, but to be conformed to Christ.

Presentation
Have chalkboard 20 on the board before class. After prayer, ask, *What is the basic difference between a thermometer and a thermostat?* (As explained in the opening illustration of this chapter, a thermometer simply registers temperature, while a thermostat controls it.) Mention the illustration given above under "Preparation," and ask, *Which of these two instruments does this type of Christian represent?* (The thermometer; they do not influence the world but are influenced by the world. They go up and down with the world around them, though they may be careful to stay a few "degrees" above it.)

What is the difference between complacency and contentment? (Both involve a lack of anxiety, but complacency is based on indifference while contentment, though it is highly concerned about problems and wrongs, refuses to be made bitter or cynical or despondent; see *Text,* p. 134.)

In what way is the overruling providence of God one of the strongest arguments against atheistic evolution? (The cardinal principle of evolution, as it is generally taught and accepted in the scientific world, is that all things, no matter how complex and intricate and interrelated, have come about entirely by chance. It is not simply the Creation and related biblical accounts that contradict evolution; every mention of a personal, powerful, and sovereign God contradicts it.)

In what way (see *Text,* p. 136) *does concern affect our opportunities for service to others and to the Lord?* (Our concern does not, of course, make or change any opportunity. But concern does make us more sensitive to opportunities and motivates us to take advantage of them for the Lord's sake.)

In what way is a Christian's relation to the Lord like the root system of a tree? (The "support system" in both cases is largely unseen, beneath the surface; *Text* p. 137; chalkboard 21. The unbeliever cannot see where the Christian's power comes from, much less understand how it operates or why.)

In what ways might a spiritual Christian and an unbeliever be compared, respectively, to an automobile engine and a stationary electric motor? (The Christian, like the automobile, has a built-in power supply, one that goes with him wherever he goes. The unbeliever, like the electric motor, has no power source in him. The motor has to be near an electrical outlet, and the unbeliever has to be in the midst of favorable circumstances, from which he must draw encouragement, support, and whatever limited satisfaction and happiness he experiences; see chalkboard 22.)

What is wrong with "trusting in our own faithfulness," (see *Text,* p. 138) *the term used by Hudson Taylor's friend?* It is a form of trusting in ourselves, not in God. The power of faith is not in the one trusting but in what, or who is trusted. It is not great faith in God that we need, but sincere faith in a great God.)

As suggested under "Preparation," why not use the latter part of this session as a sharing period? Give class members an opportunity to express blessings they have received from this study. (You may want to do this

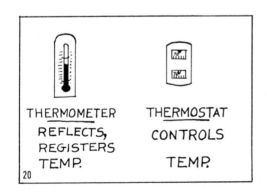

Chalkboard 20
Draw a simulated thermometer on one side of the board and a thermostat on the other. Label as indicated.

instead of a review during your thirteenth session, if you have one. Ask that comments be limited as much as possible to experiences of joy that members believe are a direct result of their obedience to the truths studied in Philippians and of their deeper submission to God's will and power. Such sharing not only encourages those who may not have had such experiences, it also reinforces—and increases—the joy of the experiences for those who had them. All of God's blessings are reinforced and enhanced when they are shared.

If you plan to have a review next session, be sure and ask for suggestions about what you will study or do. Areas that you think have been well-presented and thoroughly studied may still be unclear to some of your people. Don't take learning for granted. There is a time for sharing our needs as well as our blessings. Ask members to bring written questions to class that they would like to have discussed further.

Chalkboard 21
In most trees, the root system is at least as extensive as the branch system, though the former is never seen. The roots furnish all the support and nourishment for the rest of the tree.

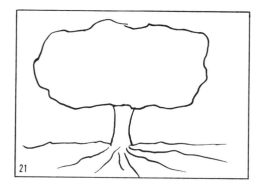

Chalkboard 22
Draw these two simple figures as shown, to illustrate outside and inner sources of energy. The automobile carries its source of energy with it.

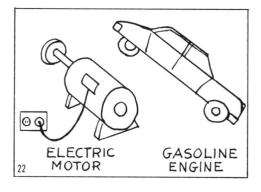

REVIEW SESSION

Be Joyful

Session Goals

You may want to review the entire course or else spend additional time on a subject, or variety of subjects, that you consider especially important. A review session is, in many ways, more difficult than others to lead meaningfully. You will need to have noted carefully the areas of major need and interest to your class, or you may find yourself rehashing topics of least significance.

A satisfactory review should include two main purposes: to highlight ideas of particular importance or urgency (or that are perhaps still unclear) and to show the entire course in greater perspective than was possible week-by-week.

Preparation

The following suggestions are general, giving broad outlines for several possible approaches to your review session. Choose the one best suited to your needs, and make your own specific plans accordingly.

Ask several discussion questions on each chapter. Determine your questions on the basis of what was emphasized in class. You may want to adapt some of the questions from the *Leader's Guide*.

Or, ask for personal testimonies from class members about how the study has been of particular help to them (if you did not do this at the end of session 12). Hopefully your members will have developed a deeper understanding and experience of true Christian joy.

Or, choose several chapters that were of special importance to your class and focus your review on these areas.

Or, discuss the written questions you asked members to bring to class at the end of last week's session.